Contents

Introduction

Welcome to the Cambridge International AS Level Information Technology Practical Skills Workbook. The aim of this Workbook is to provide you with further opportunity to practise the skills you have acquired through using the Cambridge International AS Level Information Technology Student's Book. It is designed to complement the textbook and to provide additional exercises to help you in your preparation for your examinations.

The chapters in this Practical Workbook reflect the numbering and order of practical elements and chapters in the Student's Book and the syllabus – so Chapter 8 in this Workbook supports the content in Chapter 8 of the Student's Book, which covers topic section 8 of the syllabus content. You will be writing your answers in this book, and as a guide there are generally two lines for each main point you need to cover – so if there are four lines you should mention two points in your answer, if there are two lines you should mention one point. However, if the answer requires only one word then there will be only one line. There is no set way to approach using this Workbook. You may wish to use it to supplement your learning of different topics as you work through each chapter of the textbook, or you may prefer to use it to reinforce your understanding as you prepare for your examinations. The Workbook is intended to be sufficiently flexible to suit whatever you feel is the best approach for your needs.

Any source files required to complete questions are located at:
www.hoddereducation.co.uk/cambridgeextras.

WORKBOOK

Cambridge
International AS Level

Information
Technology
Practical Skills

Graham Brown

HODDER
EDUCATION

Orders: please contact Hachette UK Distribution, Hely Hutchinson Centre, Milton Road, Didcot, Oxfordshire, OX11 7HH. Telephone: +44 (0)1235 827827. Email education@hachette.co.uk Lines are open from 9 a.m. to 5 p.m., Monday to Friday. You can also order through our website: www.hoddereducation.com

ISBN: 978 1 5104 8306 4

© Graham Brown 2022

First published in 2022 by
Hodder Education,
An Hachette UK Company
Carmelite House
50 Victoria Embankment
London EC4Y 0DZ

www.hoddereducation.com

Impression number   10 9 8 7 6 5 4 3 2 1

Year   2025 2024 2023 2022

Cover photo © cookiecutter - stock.adobe.com

Illustrations by Aptara

Typeset in India by Aptara

Printed in the UK

A catalogue record for this title is available from the British Library.

MIX
Paper from
responsible sources
FSC™ C104740

WORLD
LAND
TRUST™

8 Spreadsheets

8.1 Create a spreadsheet

1   Complete the following sentences using the correct terms from this list:

-   cell
-   cells
-   columns
-   rows

-   sheet
-   table
-   workbook
-   worksheet

A spreadsheet is a two-dimensional .... split into .... and

.... It is made up of a number of individual .... Each

.... has an address, for example: G7. A spreadsheet is sometimes called a

.... or even a .... In *Excel* many sheets can be held within a

single ....

2   Identify what the contents of a cell can contain.

A cell can hold a ....

A cell can hold a ....

A cell can hold a ....

3   A spreadsheet has been created for a company called Ben's Boxes as required. The spreadsheet looks like this:

	A	B	C	D	E
1	Ben's Boxes Sales Invoice				
2		Price	Item	Quantity	Total
3	KM Creative	$10.50	Large pack C3	2	$21.00
4	Binnaccount	$12.10	Large pack B4	5	$60.50
5	Tawara Traders	$2.65	Extra Large single D7	1	$2.65
6	Jenna's Jewellery	$8.00	Small pack A1	5	$40.00
7				Sub Total	$124.15
8	Tax rate	18%		Tax	$22.35
9				Invoice Total	$146.50

Identify the contents of the following cells and complete the sentence:

a   Cell A5 holds a ....

b   Cell D4 holds a ....

c   Cell E7 holds a ....

4   Describe the process of renaming a worksheet within a workbook.

....

....

....

....

5   Describe the process of creating a new worksheet called **Invoice** within a workbook.

....

....

....

....

8.1.1 Create the structure

6   Describe how to change the size of a spreadsheet so that it would print on A3 paper.

....

....

....

....

7   Describe how to set the orientation of a spreadsheet so that it would print in landscape.

....

....

....

....

8 Describe how to set page margins like this:

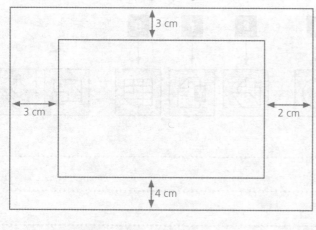

....

....

....

....

....

....

....

9 Describe how to place your name on the left in the header of the spreadsheet.

....

....

....

....

....

....

10 Identify, for each icon, the element inserted in the header or footer.

a ....

b ....

c ....

d ....

e ....

f ....

g ....

11 Describe how to display gridlines when a spreadsheet is printed or exported.

....

....

....

....

12 Describe how to display row and column headings when a spreadsheet is printed or exported.

....

....

....

....

13 Describe how to insert a cell into a spreadsheet so that it shifts the cells down.

....

....

....

14 A spreadsheet has been created and looks like this:

	A	B	C	D	E
1	Ben's Boxes Sales Invoice				
2		Price	Item	Quantity	Total
3	KM Creative	$10.50	Large pack C3	2	$21.00
4	Binnaccount	$12.10	Large pack B4	5	$60.50
5	Tawara Traders	$2.65	Extra Large single D7	1	$2.65
6	Jenna's Jewellery	$8.00	Small pack A1	5	$40.00
7				Sub Total	$124.15
8	Tax rate	18%		Tax	$22.35
9				Invoice Total	$146.50

a Describe how to insert a new row between rows 1 and 2.

....

....

....

....

b Describe how to delete row 5.

....

....

....

....

c Describe how to hide row 8.

....

....

d Practice these skills using the file **bbsi.xlsx**

15 A spreadsheet has been created and looks like this:

	A	B	C	D	E
1	Ben's Boxes Sales Invoice				
2		Price	Item	Quantity	Total
3	KM Creative	$10.50	Large pack C3	2	$21.00
4	Binnaccount	$12.10	Large pack B4	5	$60.50
5	Tawara Traders	$2.65	Extra Large single D7	1	$2.65
6	Jenna's Jewelle	$8.00	Small pack A1	5	$40.00
7				Sub Total	$124.15
8	Tax rate	18%		Tax	$22.35
9				Invoice Total	$146.50

a Describe what is wrong with this spreadsheet.

....

....

b Describe how to correct this.

....

....

....

....

16 A spreadsheet has been created and looks like this:

	A	B	C	D	E
1	Ben's Boxes Sales Invoice				
2		Price	Item	Quantity	Total
3	KM Creative	$10.50	Large pack C3	2	$21.00
4	Binnaccount	$12.10	Large pack B4	5	$60.50
5	Tawara Traders	$2.65	Extra Large single D7	1	$2.65
6	Jenna's Jewellery	$8.00	Small pack A1	5	$40.00
7				Sub Total	$124.15
8	Tax rate	18%		Tax	$22.35
9				Invoice Total	$146.50

    a   Describe how to merge cells A1 to E1.

....

....

....

    b   Practice this merge using the file **bbsi.xlsx**

17 **a**   Explain the term text wrapping in relation to a spreadsheet and why it is needed.

....

....

....

....

    b   Describe how to wrap text in a cell.

....

....

....

....

18 A spreadsheet has been created and looks like this:

	A	B	C	D	E
1	Ben's Boxes Sales Invoice				
2		Price	Item	Quantity	Total
3	KM Creative	$10.50	Large pack C3	2	$21.00
4	Binnaccount	$12.10	Large pack B4	5	$60.50
5	Tawara Traders	$2.65	Extra Large single D7	1	$2.65
6	Jenna's Jewellery	$8.00	Small pack A1	5	$40.00
7				Sub Total	$124.15
8	Tax rate	18%		Tax	$22.35
9				Invoice Total	$146.50

a Describe how to protect cells D7 to E9 with the password **BbSi**

....

....

....

....

....

....

....

....

....

....

b Test your formula using the file **bbsi.xlsx**

8.1.2 Create formulae and use functions

19 Identify the character that you place in a spreadsheet to start a formula.

....

20 Identify the mathematical operator used to calculate:

a the sum of the two numbers ....

b the difference between the two numbers ....

c the product of the two numbers ....

d the contents of one cell divided by the contents of another cell ....

e the contents of one cell to the power of the contents of another cell ....

21 Explain the difference between absolute and relative cell references.

....

....

....

....

....

22 Describe how to display the formulae used in a spreadsheet rather than the values.

....

....

....

....

23 A spreadsheet has been created and looks like this:

	A	B	C	D	E
1	Ben's Boxes Sales Invoice				
2		Price	Item	Quantity	Total
3	KM Creative	$10.50	Large pack C3	2	$21.00
4	Binnaccount	$12.10	Large pack B4	5	$60.50
5	Tawara Traders	$2.65	Extra Large single D7	1	$2.65
6	Jenna's Jewellery	$8.00	Small pack A1	5	$40.00
7				Sub Total	$124.15
8	Tax rate	18%		Tax	$22.35
9				Invoice Total	$146.50

a Identify the formula placed in cell E3. ....

b Identify the formula placed in cell E7. ....

c Identify the formula placed in cell E8. ....

d Identify the formula placed in cell E9. ....

24 A spreadsheet has been created and looks like this:

	A	B	C	D	E
1	Ben's Boxes Sales Invoice				
2		Price	Item	Quantity	Total
3	KM Creative	$10.50	Large pack C3	2	$21.00
4	Binnaccount	$12.10	Large pack B4	5	$60.50
5	Tawara Traders	$2.65	Extra Large single D7	1	$2.65
6	Jenna's Jewellery	$8.00	Small pack A1	5	$40.00
7				Sub Total	$124.15
8	Tax rate	18%		Tax	$22.35
9				Invoice Total	$146.50

a   Describe how to create a named cell in B8 which is called TAX.

....

....

....

....

....

b   Create this named cell using the file **bbsi.xlsx**

25 Is a named cell an absolute reference or a relative reference to that cell?

....

26 Explain what is meant by the term 'named range' when using a spreadsheet.

....

....

....

....

....

27 A spreadsheet has been created to calculate the pay for 5 employees of a company and looks like this:

	A	B	C
1	**Rate of pay**	£19.40	
2			
3	**Name**	**Hours worked**	**Pay**
4	David Watson	24	
5	Graham Brown	30	
6	John Reeves	22	
7	Brian Sargent	8	
8	Emily Wright	32	
9	**Total**		
10	**Average**		
11	**Maximum**		
12	**Minimum**		

a Identify the most appropriate *Excel* function to place in cell:

   i   B9 ....

   ii   B10 ....

   iii B11 ....

   iv   B12 ....

b Identify the formulae that would be entered in cell:

   i   C4 ....

   ii   B9 ....

   iii B12 ....

c Explain how to replicate the formula in cell C4 for each person.

   ....

   ....

   ....

   ....

   ....

28 Explain what is meant by the term 'function' when using a spreadsheet.

....

....

....

....

29 Explain what the following function calculates:

=SUM(A1:A3,A8,A16)

....

....

....

....

30 Explain what the following function calculates:

=SUM(Revenue)

....

....

....

....

31 Explain, identifying an equivalent formula, what the following function calculates:

=AVERAGE(C4:C7)

....

....

....

....

32 Explain what the following function calculates:

=MAX(Revenue)

....

....

....

....

33 Explain what the following function calculates:

=MIN(Revenue)

....

....

....

....

34 In a different spreadsheet, cell A4 contains the formula =INT(C9)

Explain the operation of this formula.

....

....

....

....

35 Describe the similarities and differences between the ROUNDUP and ROUNDDOWN functions.

....

....

....

....

....

36 Describe the difference between the COUNT and COUNTA functions.

....

....

....

....

....

....

37 Describe the operation of each of the formulae shown and for each identify what would be displayed in the cell:

	A
1	64.5519
2	
3	=ROUND(A1,2)
4	=ROUND(A1,0)
5	=ROUND(A1,-1)
6	=INT(A1)

a **i** Cell A3 – operation: ....

....

....

ii Result displayed: ....

b **i** Cell A4 – operation: ....

....

....

ii Result displayed: ....

c **i** Cell A5 – operation: ....

....

....

  ii Result displayed: ....

d **i** Cell A6 – operation: ....

....

....

  ii Result displayed: ....

38 Describe the reason for the formula in cell A14 and explain how it works.

	A
1	**Number of books read**
2	
3	James
4	62
5	Udoka
6	56
7	Lee
8	60
9	Jasmine
10	56
11	Karla
12	23
13	
14	=COUNTA(A3:A12)-COUNT(A3:A12)

....

....

....

....

....

....

39 A cell contains the function =COUNTIF($F$16:$F$26,"Winner")

Using cell references explain what this function does.

....

....

....

....

40 A cell contains the function =COUNTIF(Result,"Winner")

Explain what this function does.

....

....

....

....

....

41 **a** A cell contains the function =COUNTIF(Result,$D$3)

Explain what this function does.

....

....

....

....

  b Explain why $D$3 has been used rather than D3.

....

....

....

....

42 A formula will be placed in cell D2 to count the number of *Apples* in the list. It will be replicated into D3 and D4 to count the *Oranges* and *Pears*. What formula should be placed in cell D2?

	A	B	C	D
1			Number of each fruit	
2	Pear		Apple	
3	Pear		Orange	
4	Orange		Pear	
5	Pear			
6	Apple			
7	Orange			
8	Orange			
9	Orange			
10	Pear			
11	Apple			
12	Apple			
13	Apple			
14	Orange			
15	Pear			
16	Apple			
17	Pear			
18	Orange			
19	Apple			
20				

....

43 Explain the term 'nested functions'.

....

....

....

44 Explain how an `IF` function works.

....

....

....

....

....

45 a Explain the similarities and differences between the IFERROR and ISERROR functions.

....

....

....

....

....

b i Give one example of a formula where an error may be generated. Identify when this error may occur.

....

....

....

....

ii Create a formula using ISERROR to trap out this error.

....

iii Create a formula using IFERROR to trap out this error.

....

46 In a different spreadsheet, the contents of cell D7 have been validated so that it can only contain an integer (whole number) between 0 and 20. Identify four different but efficient formulae using nested IF functions to look at the contents of cell D7 and display:
 – **Low** if D7 is less than or equal to 2.
 – **Medium** if D7 is greater than 2 and less than or equal to 7.
 – **High** if D7 is greater than 7.

....

....

....

....

47 Cell D7 can only contain an integer (whole number). Identify an efficient formula using the IFS function to look at the contents of cell D7 and display:
- **Low** if D7 is less than or equal to 2.
- **Medium** if D7 is greater than 2 and less than or equal to 7.
- **High** if D7 is greater than 7.

....

48 A spreadsheet has been created and looks like this:

	A	B	C	D	E	F	G	H	I	J	K	L	M
1		Games in week 1		Games in week 2		Games in week 3		Games in week 4		Games in week 5		Games in week 6	
2	Team	Score	Win/Lose	Score	Win/Lose	Score	Win/Lose	Score	Win/Lose	Score	Win/Lose	Score	Win/Lose
3	Riders	296	Win	201	Draw	215	Win	Abandoned	Draw	230	Lose	95	Lose
4	Flyers	325	Win	201	Draw	124	Win	Abandoned	Draw	69	Win	64	Lose
5	Aces	67	Lose	Abandoned	Draw	71	Lose	62	Win	100	Lose	120	Win
6	Boomerangs	79	Win	Abandoned	Draw	280	Lose	117	Lose	Abandoned	Draw	120	Win
7	Wizards	Abandoned	Draw	342	Win	216	Draw	Abandoned	Draw	Abandoned	Draw	100	Lose
8	Mavericks	212	Lose	295	Lose	26	Lose	124	Win	73	Lose	230	Win
9	Cowboys	63	Lose	75	Lose	Abandoned	Draw	60	Lose	68	Lose	245	Lose
10	Outlanders	Abandoned	Draw	152	Lose	Abandoned	Draw	207	Lose	154	Win	Abandoned	Draw
11	Jets	72	Lose	203	Win	216	Draw	Abandoned	Draw	142	Win	Abandoned	Draw
12	Jupiters	Abandoned	Draw	89	Win	56	Lose	245	Win	130	Lose	210	Lose
13	Yorkies	Abandoned	Draw	142	Win	305	Win	147	Win	242	Win	96	Win
14	Storm	215	Win	139	Lose	317	Win	144	Lose	161	Win	250	Win

a Identify the most efficient formula that will count the number of games that were drawn but were not abandoned. Hint: Each drawn game involves 2 teams.

....

b Identify the most efficient formula that will count the number of games that were drawn but were not abandoned during each week.

Week 1 ....

Week 2 ....

Week 3 ....

Week 4 ....

Week 5 ....

Week 6 ....

c Open the file **games.xlsx**

Wrap the text in cell A16.

d Wrap the text in the merged cell L16:M16.

e Place in cell B16 your formula from part a.

f Place in cells B19 to B24 your formulae for part b.

49 A spreadsheet has been created and looks like this:

	A	B	C	D	E	F	G
1			The Manta Conservation Project				
2	Region code	Region	Total income		Date	Region code	Amount
3	AF	Africa	$81.25		13/02/2022	AF	$18.75
4	AS	Asia	$621.88		13/02/2022	AS	$187.50
5	AU	Australasia	$178.13		13/02/2022	NA	$1,247.50
6	EU	Europe	$1,345.00		13/02/2022	EU	$31.25
7	NA	North America	$1,548.13		14/02/2022	NA	$150.63
8	SA	South America	$94.69		14/02/2022	SA	$62.50
9					14/02/2022	AF	$62.50
10					14/02/2022	AS	$31.25
11					14/02/2022	EU	$18.75
12					15/02/2022	AU	$175.00
13					15/02/2022	EU	$1,250.00
14					15/02/2022	NA	$25.00
15					16/02/2022	SA	$32.19
16					16/02/2022	EU	$20.00
17					16/02/2022	NA	$125.00
18					16/02/2022	AS	$68.75
19					17/02/2022	AS	$15.63
20					18/02/2022	AS	$12.50
21					18/02/2022	AU	$3.13
22					19/02/2022	EU	$25.00
23					19/02/2022	AS	$306.25

Cell C3 contains the formula `=SUMIF($F$3:$F$23,A3,$G$3:$G$23)`

Using cell references, explain what this formula does.

....

....

....

....

....

....

50 A spreadsheet has been created and looks like this:

	A	B	C	D	E	F	G	H	I	J	K	L	M	N	O
1		Game 1		Game 2		Game 3		Game 4		Game 5		Game 6			Score greater than 200
2	Team	Score	Win/Lose	Score	Win/Lose	Score	Win/Lose	Score	Win/Lose	Score	Win/Lose	Score	Win/Lose		
3	Riders	296	Win	201	Draw	215	Win	Abandoned	Draw	230	Lose	95	Lose		
4	Flyers	325	Win	201	Draw	124	Win	Abandoned	Draw	69	Win	64	Lose		
5	Aces	67	Lose	Abandoned	Draw	71	Lose	62	Win	100	Lose	120	Win		
6	Boomerangs	79	Win	Abandoned	Draw	280	Lose	117	Lose	Abandoned	Draw	120	Win		
7	Wizards	Abandoned	Draw	342	Win	216	Draw	Abandoned	Draw	Abandoned	Draw	100	Win		
8	Mavericks	212	Lose	295	Lose	26	Lose	124	Win	73	Lose	230	Win		
9	Cowboys	63	Lose	75	Lose	Abandoned	Draw	60	Lose	68	Lose	245	Lose		
10	Outlanders	Abandoned	Draw	152	Lose	Abandoned	Draw	207	Lose	154	Win	Abandoned	Draw		
11	Jets	72	Lose	203	Win	216	Draw	Abandoned	Draw	142	Win	Abandoned	Draw		
12	Jupiters	Abandoned	Draw	89	Win	56	Lose	245	Win	130	Lose	210	Lose		
13	Yorkies	Abandoned	Draw	142	Win	305	Win	147	Win	242	Win	96	Win		
14	Storm	215	Win	139	Lose	317	Win	144	Lose	161	Win	250	Win		
15															

    a   Identify the most efficient replicable formula than can be placed in cell O3 to add, for all teams, only the scores of more than 200 in their 6 games.

....

b Identify the most efficient formula than can be placed in cell L17 to display the average score for teams who won game 6.

....

c Open the file **games.xlsx**

Place in cell O3 your formula from part a. Replicate this formula for all teams. Place in cell L17 your formula from part b.

51 Explain, including the function used in *Excel*, the terms mean, median and mode.

Mean: ....

....

Median: ....

....

Mode: ....

....

52 A student has to create a nested IF statement to display messages depending upon a test score (a whole number between 0 and 10) which is held in cell C1. If the score is:
- 3–5 inclusive the message **Grade C** should be displayed
- less than 3 the message **Grade D** should be displayed
- greater than 8 the message **Grade A** should be displayed
- 6,7, or 8 the message **Grade B** should be displayed.

The student created the following formula:

=IF(C1<6,"Grade C",IF(C1<3,"Grade D",IF(C1=6,"Grade B",IF(C1=7,"Grade B",IF(C1=8,"Grade B","Grade A")))))

a Explain why this formula does not work.

....

....

....

....

b Create a more efficient formula to solve this problem.

....

....

53 Explain the differences between HLOOKUP, VLOOKUP and XLOOKUP functions.

....

....

....

....

....

....

....

....

54 A cell contains the function

=VLOOKUP(X4,$F$3:$H$16,3,0)

Explain what this function does.

....

....

....

....

....

55 The last parameter of a HLOOKUP function can be 0 or 1. Explain what these values represent.

....

....

....

....

....

....

56 A cell contains the function

=XLOOKUP(X4,$F$2:$F$16,$D$2:$D$16,"Data corrupt",0,1)

Explain what this function does.

....

....

....

....

....

57 A spreadsheet has been created and looks like this:

	A	B	C	D	E	F
1	Contract number			Contractor's name		
2						
3	Contractor			Current contract		
4	Payroll	Name		Company name	Contract number	Duration in days
5	TLI004	Lyra Ramsey		Binnaccount	00047	120
6	TLI005	Ida Rosales		Tawara Trucks	00048	62
7	TLI006	Raheel Richard		KM Creative	00079	2
8	TLI007	May Piper		Jenna's Jewellery	00050	21
9	TLI008	Darcey Frost		Amat Supplies	00077	3
10	TLI009	Aaminah Glass		Binnaccount	00052	20
11	TLI010	Huzaifah Freeman		Tawara Zoo	00053	12
12	TLI011	Lilly-Grace Clemons		Tawara Traders	00065	7
13	TLI012	Jaheim Deleon		Binnaccount	00055	7
14	TLI013	Taliyah Field		Tawara Traders	00074	5
15	TLI014	Amanpreet Holding		Binnaccount	00057	7

The contract number is entered in cell B1.

a Identify the most efficient formula than can be placed in cell E1 to display the name of the contractor for that contract or display **Wrong contract ID** if the contract number entered is not found.

....

b Open the file **contractor.xlsx**

Place in cell E1 your formula from part a. Test this formula to make sure it works for all contract numbers.

58 Explain the INDEX and MATCH functions.

INDEX: ....

....

....

MATCH: ....

....

....

59 A cycle race has a time trial where each racer completes the same course, but they all start at different times. The racers details are stored in a spreadsheet like this:

	A	B	C	D
1	Locate the name of the racer:			
2	Racer finishing position			
3	Racer name			
4				
5	Entry number	Starting order	Name	Finishing position
6	Racer00001	30	Mohamed Abdelmeged	111
7	Racer00002	77	Misha Laeeq	67
8	Racer00003	32	Isra Wattanapanit	19
9	Racer00004	14	Billy Green	43
10	Racer00007	125	Kanya Charoenkul	77

There are 156 racers (so the data is held between rows 6 and 161).

The position the racer finished the race will be entered into cell C2.

a Identify the most efficient formula than can be placed in cell C3 to display the name of the racer who finished in that position.

....

....

b Open the file **race.xlsx**

Place in cell C3 your formula from part a. Use this formula to identify the name of the racer who finished in 1st place.

Name: ....

c Use this formula to identify the name of the racer who finished in 84th place.

Name: ....

60 Explain the CONCATENATE function.

....

....

61 A spreadsheet has been created and looks like this:

	A	B
1	Full name:	Brown: Philippa Louise
2		
3	First Name:	
4	Middle name:	
5	Family name:	
6	Length of full name:	

A person's name has been entered in cell B1. Formulae will be placed in cells B3 to B6 to display each part of this name and the length of this full name. This name will not be changed.

a Identify the most efficient formula for cell B3 to extract the first name (**Philippa**) from cell B1.

....

b Identify the most efficient formula for cell B4 to extract the middle name (**Louise**) from cell B1.

....

c Identify a different formula (using a different function) for cell B4.

....

d Identify the most efficient formula for cell B5.

....

e Identify a different formula (using a different function) for cell B5.

....

f Identify the most efficient formula for cell B6 to count the number of characters in the full name.

....

62 A spreadsheet has been created and looks like this:

	A	B
1	First Name:	Karla
2	Middle name:	Marie
3	Family name:	Brown
4		
5	Full name:	

A person's name is placed in cells B1, B2 and B3. A formula will be placed in cell B5 to display the full name of the person in this format **Brown: Karla Marie**

a Identify the most efficient formula that uses a function for cell B5.

....

b Identify the most efficient formula that does not use a function for cell B5.

....

63 A spreadsheet has data in cell X5. *Excel* has three functions that are used to test the type of data held/displayed in a cell. Identify these three functions and how they are used with reference to cell X5. Explain each function.

Function 1: ....

....

....

Function 2: ....

....

....

Function 3: ....

....

....

64 Functions can be used to turn strings into capitals or lower-case letters.

a Identify the most efficient formula to change a string held in cell X5 into capital characters.

....

b Identify the most efficient formula to change a string held in cell X5 into lower-case characters.

....

65 Explain the purpose of the EXACT function.

....

....

66 Cell X5 holds the text **Hello**

Another cell contains the function:

=CODE(X5)

Explain what this function does.

....

....

....

67 Cell Y5 holds the number 65. Another cell contains the function:

=CHAR(Y5)

Explain what this function does.

....

....

....

....

68 Explain the purpose of the DEC2HEX function.

....

....

69 Explain the purpose of the HEX2BIN function.

....

....

70 A cell contains the function:

=WEEKDAY(T5)

Explain what this function does and what must be held in cell T5 in order for this function to work.

....

....

....

....

71 A spreadsheet has been created and looks like this:

	A	B
1	01 September 2001	14 April 2022
2		

Cell A3 contains the function:

=DATEDIF(A1,B1,"D")

a Explain what this function does.

....

....

....

....

b Identify two changes that could be made to the final parameter. For each of these changes explain what the cell will display.

i Change made: ....

Displayed: ....

ii Change made: ....

Displayed: ....

72 Explain the purpose of the HOUR function.

....

....

....

....

73 Explain the purpose of the MINUTE function.

....

....

....

....

74 Explain the purpose of the SECOND function.

....

....

....

....

75 Identify the feature used to create a drop-down list of options to restrict data entry within a cell.

....

76 A spreadsheet has been created and looks like this:

	A	B	C	D	E
1	Ben's Boxes Sales Invoice				
2		Price	Item	Quantity	Total
3	KM Creative	$10.50	Large pack C3	2	$21.00
4	Binnaccount	$12.10	Large pack B4	5	$60.50
5	Tawara Traders	$2.65	Extra Large single D7	1	$2.65
6	Jenna's Jewellery	$8.00	Small pack A1	5	$40.00
7				Sub Total	$124.15
8	Tax rate	18%		Tax	$22.35
9				Invoice Total	$146.50

a Identify the formatting applied to cell B3. ....

b Identify the formatting applied to cell B8. ....

77 Cell A1 of a spreadsheet holds the date 23 September 2025. Cells A3 to A5 hold the following formulae:

	A
3	=TEXT(A1, "dd mm yy")
4	=TEXT(A1, "dd mmm yyyy")
5	=TEXT(A1, "dd mmmm yyyy")

a State what will be displayed in cell A3. ....

b State what will be displayed in cell A4. ....

c State what will be displayed in cell A5. ....

78 A spreadsheet has been created and looks like this:

	A	B	C	D	E
1	Hotels in Ellmau with rooms available on 3rd March				
2					
3			Type of Room		
4			Single	Double	Family
5	Hotel name	AktivHotel Hochfilzer	None	1	None
6		Alpenpension Claudia	3	5	9
7		Appartment Fuchs	8	1	2
8		Appartmenthaus Bambi	5	None	5
9		Apparthotel Tom Sojer	2	6	4
10		Ferienappartments Landhof	1	9	3
11		Haus Harmony	4	10	8
12		Hotel Alte Post	None	2	10
13		Hotel Der Bär	None	9	1
14		Kaiserblick	5	4	6
15		Kaiserhof	None	5	None
16		Landhotel Föhrenhof	3	None	7
17		Pension Rainer	8	None	7
18		Sporthotel	8	7	4

a Describe the formatting applied to the merged cell A5:E1.

....

....

....

....

b Describe the formatting applied to cell A5.

....

....

....

....

c Describe the formatting applied to cell C4.

....

....

d Describe the formatting applied to cell B5.

....

79 a Cell A1 in this spreadsheet will be formatted as an integer. Explain what happens to the contents of the cell and what is displayed in the cell.

	A
1	96.62459

....

....

....

b What would be displayed in cell A1 if it was formatted:

i as an integer ....

ii to 1 decimal place ....

iii to 2 decimal places ....

iv to 3 decimal places ....

80 Explain the purpose of conditional formatting.

....

....

....

....

8.2 Test a spreadsheet

81 Identify 4 column headings used in the creation of a test plan.

....

....

....

....

82 Name the three types of test data used within a test plan.

....

....

....

83 Identify which columns of a test plan hold data that is entered before the test and which hold data entered after the test. Write your answers in this table.

Entered before test:	Entered after the test:

8.3 Use a spreadsheet

84 When searching a spreadsheet using AutoFilter mathematical operators can be used. Explain what each operator means:

a   =

....

b   <>

....

c   >

....

d   <

....

e   >=

....

f   <=

....

85 Explain how you would perform a wildcard search in *Excel*.

....

....

....

....

86 The following are extracts from a spreadsheet:

Extract i

	A	B	C
	First name	Surname	Tutor group
1			
2	Emily	Wright	11XSJR
3	Alexande	Terry	11YCAL
4	Sophie	Clinch	11YVM
5	George	Arnold	11YVM
6	Rachel	Noles	11XSJR
7	Thomas	Kleider	11XSJR

Extract ii

	A	B	C
	First name	Surname	Tutor group
1			
2	Alexande	Terry	11YCAL
3	Emily	Wright	11XSJR
4	George	Arnold	11YVM
5	Rachel	Noles	11XSJR
6	Sophie	Clinch	11YVM
7	Thomas	Kleider	11XSJR

Extract iii

	A	B	C
	First name	Surname	Tutor group
1			
2	George	Arnold	11YVM
3	Sophie	Clinch	11YVM
4	Thomas	Kleider	11XSJR
5	Rachel	Noles	11XSJR
6	Alexande	Terry	11YCAL
7	Emily	Wright	11XSJR

Extract iv

	A	B	C
	First name	Surname	Tutor group
1			
2	Sophie	Clinch	11YVM
3	George	Arnold	11YVM
4	Alexande	Terry	11YCAL
5	Emily	Wright	11XSJR
6	Rachel	Noles	11XSJR
7	Thomas	Kleider	11XSJR

a Describe for each extract, the sorting applied to the data:

i ....

....

ii ....

....

iii ....

....

iv ....

....

b Identify the feature used to make the text in cells A1 and C1 fit within the column width.

....

87 Identify two methods that may prevent the loss of data integrity when sorting data in a spreadsheet.

Method 1: ....

....

Method 2: ....

....

88 A spreadsheet shown in 88i been sorted in ascending order of **Surname** to get the spreadsheet shown in 88ii.

Fig. 88i		
	A	B	C
1	First name	Surname	Tutor group
2	Emily	Wright	11XSJR
3	Alexander	Terry	11YCAL
4	Sophie	Clinch	11YVMA
5	George	Arnold	11YVMA
6	Rachel	Noles	11XSJR
7	Thomas	Kleider	11XSJR

Fig. 88ii		
	A	B	C
1	First name	Surname	Tutor group
2	Emily	Arnold	11XSJR
3	Alexander	Clinch	11YCAL
4	Sophie	Kleider	11YVMA
5	George	Noles	11YVMA
6	Rachel	Terry	11XSJR
7	Thomas	Wright	11XSJR

a Explain what is wrong with this sorted data.

....

....

....

b Describe how this issue could have been avoided.

....

....

....

89 Describe the purpose of a pivot table.

....

....

....

....

90 A spreadsheet shown in 90i has been sorted in ascending order of **Surname** to get the spreadsheet shown in 90ii.

Fig. 90i		
	A	B	C
1	First name	Surname	Tutor group
2	Emily	Wright	11XSJR
3	Alexander	Terry	11YCAL
4	Sophie	Clinch	11YVMA
5	George	Arnold	11YVMA
6	Rachel	Noles	11XSJR
7	Thomas	Kleider	11XSJR

Fig. 90ii		
	A	B	C
1	George	Arnold	11YVMA
2	Sophie	Clinch	11YVMA
3	Thomas	Kleider	11XSJR
4	Rachel	Noles	11XSJR
5	First name	Surname	Tutor group
6	Alexander	Terry	11YCAL
7	Emily	Wright	11XSJR

a   Explain what is wrong with this sorted data.

....

....

....

b   Describe how this issue could have been avoided.

....

....

....

91 a   Describe how to export spreadsheet data into a PDF file.

....

....

....

b   Explain how a spreadsheet is affected when it is turned into a PDF file.

....

....

....

....

8.4 Automate operations with a spreadsheet

92 Describe the purpose of using a macro in a spreadsheet.

....

....

....

....

....

....

8.5 Graphs and charts

93 For each of the following chart types, explain what that chart type is used for. Give one example of an appropriate use for each chart type.

a Pie chart

What is it used for? ....

....

....

Example of appropriate use: ....

....

b Bar chart

What is it used for? ....

....

....

Example of appropriate use: ....

....

c Line graph

What is it used for? ....

....

....

Example of appropriate use: ....

....

....

94 Identify **all** the following graphs and charts that would be the most suitable for displaying:

a The time taken to travel different distances. ....

b The percentage of people with different shoe sizes. ....

c A comparison of the annual sales figures for three different offices in a company. ....

d The number of apples eaten this month by four students. ....

e The amount spent in one year on health care by ten companies. ....

f The height compared to the weight of all the students in a class. ....

g Whether students travel to school by bike, car or walking. ....

A

B

C

D

E

F

G

95 Which type of graph or chart would best:

a Display the temperature of water as it is heated with time. ....

b Compare the number of items bought by 24 people in one month. ....

c Compare fractions of a whole. ....

d Display the percentage of boys and girls in a class. ....

96 The following data will be used to create a new chart showing the amount of water filling a bath.

Volume of water in litres	0	6	13	21	30	40	51	62	74
Time in seconds	0	20	40	60	80	100	120	140	160

    a   State the type of chart that will be most appropriate. ....

....

    b   Explain why this is the most appropriate type. ....

....

....

    c   Explain how this chart would be structured. ....

....

....

97 A spreadsheet extract looks like this:

	G	H	I
12		**Average Temperature**	
13	**Town**	**January**	**February**
14	Amarta	-4.3	-4.7
15	Bengamzi	2.1	2.3
16	Choyen	-0.02	2.1

Identify any cells in row 15 of this spreadsheet that are:

    a   contiguous ....

....

....

    b   non-contiguous ....

....

....

98 Identify the key (on the keyboard) that is held down when you select non-contiguous data using the mouse.

....

99 Explain why secondary axes would be needed for some graphs and charts.

....

....

....

....

....

....

....

....

100 Identify what values may be changed in the secondary axis of a comparative line graph to improve its readability.

....

....

....

101 Describe the steps required to extract only the **Programmer** segment on this chart:

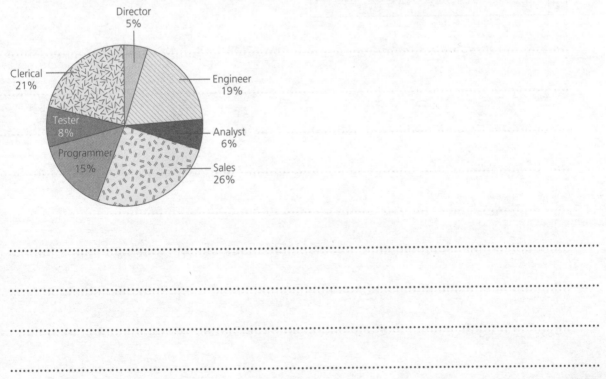

....

....

....

9 Modelling

9.3 Using what-if analysis

1 Explain the term 'Goal Seek' in relation to a spreadsheet.

....

....

....

....

....

....

....

2 For this spreadsheet, explain how you would use 'Goal Seek' to set cell D4 to the value 250 by changing the value in cell A3.

	A	B	C	D
1				
2	Cost per hour	Number of hours	Fixed cost	Total cost
3		14.3	$41.25	

....

....

....

....

....

....

....

Cambridge International AS Level Information Technology Practical Skills Workbook

10 Databases and file concepts

10.1 Database basics

10.1.1 Database types

1 Explain the terms database and database program.

Database ....

....

....

Database program ....

....

....

2 Describe the following terms in relation to a database:

a File ....

....

....

....

....

b Field ....

....

c Record ....

....

....

d Flat-file database ....

....

....

e Relational database ....

....

....

....

....

f Table ....

....

....

....

g Primary key ....

....

....

....

h Foreign key ....

....

....

....

....

3 Describe the reasons for using a relational database rather than a flat-file database.

....

....

....

....

....

....

4 Label the parts of this database.

Teacher_ID	Forename	Surname	Subject	Room
GBR	Graham	Brown	ICT	60
GBA	Graham	Barney	Science	14
JKW	Jennie	Kwong	English	42
PTY	Paul	Tyrell	Science	13
SJR	Sarah	Jordan	English	43

(a) →

(b) →

(c)

a ....

b ....

c ....

10.1.2 Data types

5 **a** Apart from numeric data, name the other **two** main data types used in database fields.

  i ....

  ii ....

  b Name and describe four sub-types of numeric data.

  i Name: ....

  Description: ....

  ....

  ....

  ii Name: ....

  Description: ....

  ....

    iii Name: ....

        Description: ....

        ....

        ....

    iv Name: ....

        Description: ....

        ....

        ....

6 Explain why a spreadsheet such as *Excel* is not suitable for database tasks.

....

....

....

....

....

....

10.1.3 Relationship types

7 Name and describe three types of relationship used in a relational database.

    a Name: ....

        Description: ....

        ....

        ....

    b Name: ....

        Description: ....

        ....

        ....

c Name: ....

Description: ....

....

....

....

....

10.1.4 Key fields

8 Describe the following terms in relation to a database:

a Primary key ....

....

....

....

b Foreign key ....

....

....

....

c Compound key ....

....

....

....

9 Name the type of field in a table that will point to the primary key field in another table.

....

10.1.5 Entity relationship diagrams

10 Name and describe three component parts of an entity relationship diagram.

a Name: ....

Description: ....

....

b Name: ....

Description: ....

....

c Name: ....

Description: ....

....

11 Identify the types of relationship shown in the following ERDs:

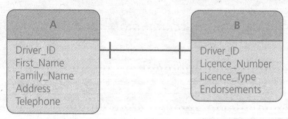

a ....

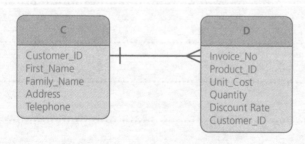

b ....

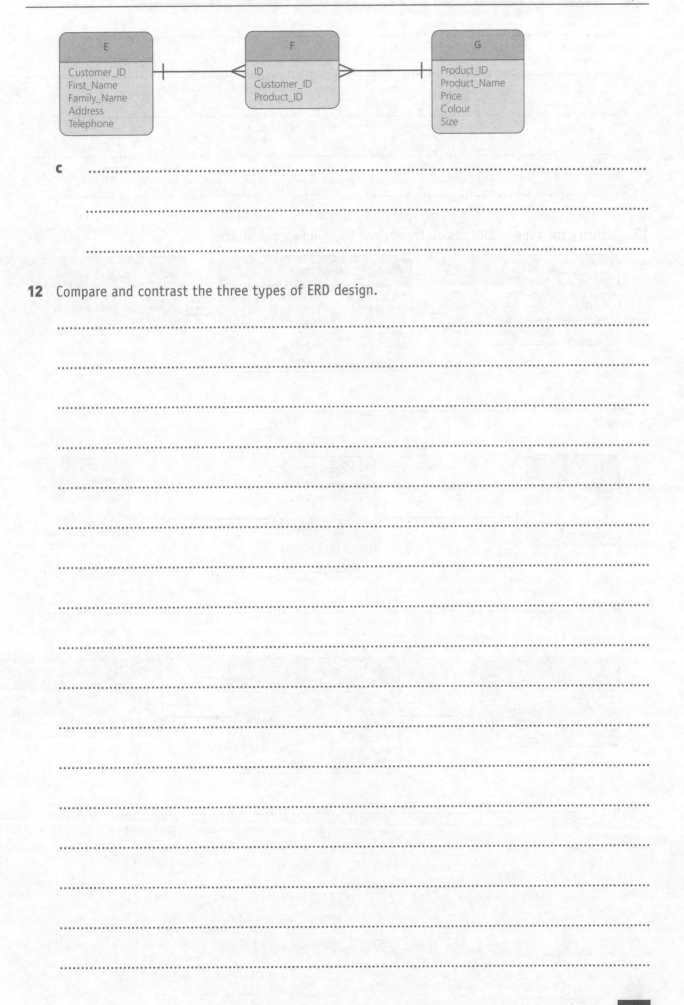

c ....

....

....

12 Compare and contrast the three types of ERD design.

....

....

....

....

....

....

....

....

....

....

....

....

....

....

....

....

....

....

....

....

13 Identify the type of ERD design for each of the following diagrams.

Site		
Site_Code	Alphanumeric	5 PK
Site_Name	Alphanumeric	34
Site_Address	Alphanumeric	150
Telephone	Alphanumeric	13

Employees		
Payroll_Number	Alphanumeric	8 PK
First_Name	Alphanumeric	30
Family_Name	Alphanumeric	36
Address	Alphanumeric	150
Job_Code	Alphanumeric	2 FK
Site_Code	Alphanumeric	5 FK

Jobs		
Job_Code	Alphanumeric	2 PK
Job_Description	Alphanumeric	60
Rate_of_Pay	Currency	2 dp

a ....

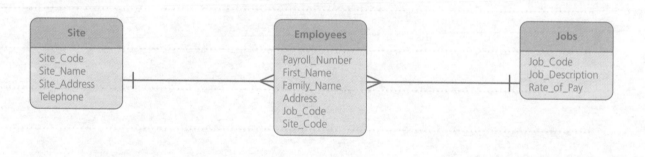

b ....

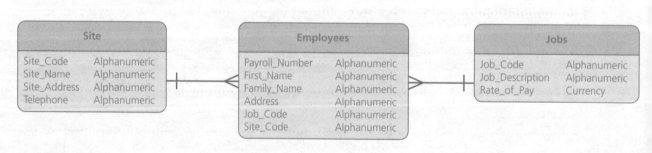

c ....

10.2 Designing the database structure

14 Identify three criteria used when deciding entity and attribute names.

a ....

b ....

c ....

15 State what an entity name in an ERD may be used for when creating a database.

....

16 State what an attribute name in an ERD may be used for when creating a database.

....

17 Explain how you would change a conceptual ERD into a logical ERD.

....

....

18 Explain how you would change a logical ERD into a physical ERD.

....

....

10.3 Creating the database structure

19 Describe how you would create a database structure from a physical ERD.

....

....

....

....

....

....

....

....

....

....

....

20 Explain the term referential integrity.

....

....

....

....

....

....

....

....

21 Explain how to change the format of a field with a Boolean data type in *Access* from Yes/No to On/Off.

....

....

....

....

....

22 Name and describe the two methods of verification that could be used when new data is typed into a database.

Method 1 ....

Description 1 ....

....

Method 2 ....

Description 2 ....

....

10.5 Querying the database

23 Name the type of query from the following list that would be used to perform each database query.

- – Simple query
- – Crosstab query
- – Find duplicates query
- – Find unmatched query

a Find all customers called **Brown**

....

b Find all customers who had placed more than one order.

....

c Find a list of all customers whose name starts with **S**

....

d Find the average cost of all invoices from all customers.

....

e Find a list of customers who do not live in Tawara.

....

24 Identify the operator used within a query to find numeric data that is:

a Equal to ....

b Greater than ....

c Less than ....

d Greater than or equal to ....

e Less than or equal to ....

f Not equal to ....

25 Identify the criteria would be placed in a query to extract records with values between 20% and 40% inclusive.

....

26 Identify the criteria would be placed in a query to extract records where the items are coloured blue, black or white.

....

27 Identify the criteria would be placed in a query to extract records where the items are **not** coloured blue.

....

28 Identify the criteria would be placed in a query to extract records where the items contain the word **wood**

....

29 Identify the criteria would be placed in a query to extract records where the date was after **23 January 2023** and before **17 March 2024**

....

30 Identify the criteria would be placed in a query to extract records where the time was between **8am** and **5pm**

....

31 Identify the criteria would be placed in a query to extract records that are blank (do not hold any data).

....

32 Compare and contrast a static parameter query and a dynamic parameter query.

....

....

....

....

....

....

....

....

....

....

....

....

33 Explain the operation of the formula in the **Discount** field of this query:

Field:	Discount	
Table:	Customer	
Sort:		
Show:	☑	
Criteria:	> = [Enter the lower discount rate] And < = [Enter the higher discount rate]	
or:		

....

....

....

....

....

....

....

....

....

....

....

34 Explain the operation of the formula in the **Order_Date** field of this query:

Field:	Order_Date	
Table:	Customer	
Sort:		
Show:	☑	
Criteria:	>[Start date] And <[End date]	
or:		

....

....

....

....

....

....

....

....

35 Explain the term 'nested query'.

....

....

....

....

....

36 Describe this query:

Field:	Total: [Sales_Price]-[Discount]	
Table:		
Sort:		
Show:	☑	
Criteria:		
or:		

....

....

....

....

....

....

37 Describe this query:

Field:	Duration: [End_Date]-[Start_Date]	
Table:		
Sort:		
Show:	☑	
Criteria:		
or:		

....

....

....

....

....

....

38 A field called **Type** will be calculated at runtime. It will extract the first 2 characters of a field called **Code** and if these contain the string **TR** it will hold the string **Tree** or if the first 2 characters of the **Code** field contain **SH** it will hold the string **Shrub**, or if neither of these strings are found it will hold **Code Error**

Identify the formula that will be entered into the **Field** box of a query to get these results.

....

....

39 Describe this query:

Field:	Price_per_sq_m: [Price]/([Length]*[Width])
Table:	
Sort:	
Show:	☑
Criteria:	
or:	

....

....

....

....

....

....

....

40 A database is being created using data imported into a single table from two different sources. Some of the data may be duplicated.

Explain how a find duplicates query can be used to help you normalise the database to 3NF.

....

....

....

....

....

....

....

....

....

....

....

....

41 a Describe a calculated control.

....

....

....

b Explain the differences between a calculated control and a calculated field.

....

....

....

....

42 Identify four functions used to summarise data that can be placed in a calculated control.

a ....

b ....

c ....

d ....

10.6 Sorting and grouping data

43 Compare and contrast grouped data and sorted data within an *Access* report.

....

....

....

....

....

....

....

....

....

10.7 Creating a data entry form

44 Explain the purpose of a data entry form.

....

....

....

....

....

45 Name the type of questions that, where possible, should be used on a database form.

....

46 Identify three items from the following list, by circling them, that would be suitable for use on a database form with closed questions.

a   Text box

b   Option group with radio (option) buttons

c List box (drop down list) with limit to list

d Drop down list without limit to list

e Tick Box (Check box)

f Combo box

47 Explain the purpose of navigation buttons on a database form.

....

....

....

....

....

48 Identify the features of a well-designed data entry form.

....

....

....

....

....

....

49 Explain the difference between a list box and a combo box on a data entry form.

....

....

....

....

....

50 Explain, giving an example, the purpose of a sub-form.

....

....

....

....

....

....

10.8 Designing a switchboard

51 Describe the purpose, use and design of a switchboard in a database.

....

....

....

....

....

....

....

....

....

....

....

....

52 Draw a circle around three database items from the following list that would be used to create a switchboard.

a Query

b Table

c Report

d   Form

e   Grouped report

10.10 Normalising data

53 Describe the purpose of normalisation.

....

....

....

....

....

54 Describe a database normalised to 0NF.

....

....

....

....

55 Identify five rules for a database normalised to 1NF.

a   ....

....

b   ....

....

c   ....

....

d   ....

....

e   ....

....

56 Identify the rule for changing a database from 2NF to 3NF.

....

....

....

....

10.11 Creating a data dictionary

57 Identify eight components of a data dictionary.

a ....

b ....

c ....

d ....

e ....

f ....

g ....

h ....

58 Identify two components of a data dictionary that can be calculated from given data files.

a ....

b ....

10.12 File and data management

59 Describe the difference between proprietary file formats and generic file formats.

....

....

....

....

....

....

....

....

....

....

60 Identify three generic file formats used for text files.

    a ....

    b ....

    c ....

61 Identify three generic file formats used for image files.

    a ....

    b ....

    c ....

62 Identify a generic file format used for audio files.

....

63 Identify two generic file formats used for website authoring.

    a ....

    b ....

64 Identify two generic file formats used for compressed files.

    a ....

    b ....

11 Sound and video editing

11.1 Video editing

1   Identify the two most common aspect ratios used for video editing.

   a ....

   b ....

2   Explain the term 'to trim' a video.

   ....

   ....

3   Explain why subtitles may be added to a video clip.

   ....

   ....

   ....

   ....

   ....

   ....

   ....

   ....

   ....

   ....

   ....

4 Explain the term 'to splice' a video clip.

....

....

....

....

5 Explain the term 'caption' when related to a video clip.

....

....

....

....

6 Explain how you would show the difference between captions and subtitles in a video clip.

....

....

....

....

....

7 Explain the purpose and use of credits in a video clip.

....

....

....

....

....

....

8 Explain why fading effects may be used for video clips.

....

....

....

....

....

....

....

9 Explain the purpose of 'pan and zoom' in a video clip.

....

....

....

....

10 Describe the function of a codec with regard to video files.

....

....

....

....

....

....

....

....

11 Identify the feature used to make a video look very old by turning a colour video into brown and white.

....

....

12 Describe the difference between 'lossy' and 'lossless' file compression for both video and audio files.

....

....

11.2 Audio editing

13 **a** Explain the term 'DC offset' with regard to audio files.

....

....

....

....

....

....

....

....

b Describe how to remove DC offset from an audio clip.

....

....

....

....

....

14 Explain why fade in and fade out effects may be used for audio clips.

....

....

....

....

....

....

....

15 Explain how to mix down a stereo clip into mono using *Audacity*.

....

....

....

....

16 Identify the feature used to make a track louder.

....

17 Two audio clips will be spliced to make a single clip. Explain why the pitch of one of the audio clips may need to be changed.

....

....

....

....

18 Explain how noise reduction can improve an audio clip and the limitations of using noise reduction.

....

....

....

....

19 Explain the term 'reverb' and how it can be used on an audio clip of a voice-over.

....

....

....

....

....

....

....

....

20 Explain the terms high-pass filter and low-pass filter.

....

....

....

....

....

....

....

....

21 Explain the terms 'echo' and 'decay'.

....

....

....

....

22 Name two units used to measure audio sampling rate.

....

....

23 Explain the term sampling resolution for an audio file.

....

....

....

....

Reinforce learning and deepen understanding of the practical elements covered in the Cambridge International AS Level Information Technology syllabus (9626); an ideal course companion or homework book for use throughout the course.

» Support students' learning with extra practice questions tailored to topics in the Student's Book.

» Keep track of students' work with ready-to-go write-in exercises.

» Ensure all topics are fully understood with practice activities that can be set in class or as homework.

Cambridge International AS Level

Information Technology

Graham Brown
Brian Sargent

Use with *Cambridge International AS Level Information Technology Student's Book*

9781510483057

For over 25 years we have been trusted by Cambridge schools around the world to provide quality support for teaching and learning. For this reason we have been selected by Cambridge Assessment International Education as an official publisher of endorsed material for their syllabuses.

This resource is endorsed by Cambridge Assessment International Education

✓ Provides learner support for the AS Level content of the Cambridge International AS & A Level Information Technology syllabus (9626) for examination from 2022

✓ Has passed Cambridge International's rigorous quality-assurance process

✓ Developed by subject experts

✓ For Cambridge schools worldwide

HODDER EDUCATION

e: education@hachette.co.uk
w: hoddereducation.com

ISBN 978-1-5104-8306-4

9 781510 483064

MIX
Paper from responsible sources
FSC™ C104740